Sight and Sound in Minecraft

Adam Hellebuyck and **Michael Medvinsky**

CHERRY LAKE
Publishing

Published in the United States of America by Cherry Lake Publishing
Ann Arbor, Michigan
www.cherrylakepublishing.com

Reading Adviser: Marla Conn, MS, Ed, Literacy Specialist, Read-Ability, Inc.

Photo Credits: © Adam Hellebuyck and Michael Medvinsky/Cover, 1, 11, 16; © LightField Studios/Shutterstock.com, 5; © Subphoto/Shutterstock.com, 7; © virtusincertus/flickr, 9; © Shadowman39/flickr, 13; © wavebreakmedia/Shutterstock.com, 15; © Dima Moroz/Shutterstock.com, 17; © Alfa Photostudio/Shutterstock.com, 19; © Marzolino/Shutterstock.com, 21; © Irina Timokhina/Shutterstock.com, 23; © katacarix / Shutterstock.com, 25; © mrwynd/flickr, 26; © Wesley Fryer/flickr, 27; © SpeedKingz/Shutterstock.com, 29

Graphic Element Credits: © Ohn Mar/Shutterstock.com, back cover, multiple interior pages; © Dmitrieva Katerina/Shutterstock.com, back cover, multiple interior pages; © advent/Shutterstock.com, back cover, front cover, multiple interior pages; © Visual Generation/Shutterstock.com, multiple interior pages; © anfisa focusova/Shutterstock.com, front cover, multiple interior pages; © Babich Alexander/Shutterstock.com, back cover, front cover, multiple interior pages;

Library of Congress Cataloging-in-Publication Data has been filed and is available at catalog.loc.gov

Printed in the United States of America
Corporate Graphics

Table of Contents

INTRODUCTION

People often show what they are feeling or thinking by creating art. Art comes in many forms. It can be visual (seen with the eyes), **audible** (heard with the ears), physical (touched), or a combination of all three. Some artists create interactive art. This is art that changes when people interact with it. You can make your own art in all these styles in *Minecraft*. Let's discover how!

Art is experienced in many different ways.

CHAPTER ONE

Archaeology: Cave Paintings

Art is one of the earliest forms of communication. Humans have used visual art to share their ideas and feelings for thousands of years. Some of the first pieces of visual art were cave paintings. During the **Paleolithic** era, early humans painted animals, other humans, and scenes from nature inside caves. Over time, this art form evolved into the art that you see in museums and the **graffiti** you see on the streets.

Archaeologists are not sure why early people made cave paintings. Most archaeologists believe the paintings were made for a specific reason. Some believe the paintings were part of a religious ritual. Others think the paintings were a way to communicate ideas. What thoughts, ideas, and feelings would you like to communicate? Think about this as you design your own version of a cave painting in *Minecraft*. Where would you

Prehistoric cave paintings are found all around the world. This painting was found in Indonesia and is estimated to be about 3,000 to 5,000 years old!

start your painting? Would you find the perfect cave already in the game, or would you carve one yourself into a mountain? What materials would you use to make your art? Would you use different types of stone or clay like early humans?

Visual art has certainly changed since Paleolithic times. Today, you see many types of art made out of different materials. Some are made out of tiny tiles, colored glass, and stone. These are called mosaics. Some art is made out of recycled material. There is also art that's made out of thread. Many cultures practice the art of weaving. These cultures would

If you needed a certain paint color, you'd go to the store. Early humans did not have this luxury. They made their own paint by using the materials found in nature. For example, they'd use leftover charcoal from a fire to make black paint. Sometimes, they would even chew the charcoal, or other material, and spit it out. They would place their hand or other object, like leaf or feather, and spit around it to create different outlines. They used other materials to paint, including twigs, horsehair, and feathers. As you make your own cave paintings in *Minecraft*, what unique materials could you use?

Some *Minecraft* users recreate famous buildings down to the paintings and statues inside. This user recreated the Pantheon in Rome!

often weave thread into **intricate** patterns to cover their floors. These woven carpets would usually be made out of wool. People in the past and also today would often hang carpets on walls as decorations. These are called tapestries.

You can make your own tapestries in *Minecraft* by building banners. These banners can have dozens of different designs. You can also make your own carpets in *Minecraft*. Try to mix wool blocks with different dyes, like yellow dye from dandelions or rose red from roses. You can then place these wool blocks on the ground in different patterns. What types of patterns can you use to make a carpet or banner for your home or other building in *Minecraft*?

Similar to *Minecraft* artists, some artists in the real world make colored dyes and paints from plants!

SCIENCE

Many artists use materials they find in the environment to create their art. For instance, wool from sheep is often used in art. Long ago, gathering wool from these sheep was no easy task. Sheep then were wild. They had large horns and were significantly smaller in size. This made them dangerous and hard to catch. Over time, humans **domesticated** the animal. They did this by breeding sheep to be larger and calmer. In science, this is called selective breeding, or artificial selection.

Artists have also collected dyes from nature. Purple was one of the hardest colors for artists to make during ancient times. Purple dye was made by crushing murex, a tiny snail. This snail was only found in certain areas along the coasts. Each snail only gave a little dye, so artists needed thousands of snails to make their creations. These snails do not exist in *Minecraft*, but lapis lazuli dye does, and it is a rare dye in the game. The dye can only be made by mining lapis lazuli underground, which is hard to find. This makes it as rare as purple dye in the real world. Have you ever found and used lapis lazuli in your art creations?

Minecraft paintings can be used for decoration or to keep a secret room hidden!

CHAPTER TWO

Music: From Communication to Feeling

People also express themselves through music. Some of the earliest music used repeated sounds in a series of patterns. This is called rhythm. Rhythmic music was one of the earliest forms of long-distance communication. Prehistoric civilizations, especially ones who lived in forested areas, used drums and logs to perform rhythmic patterns to relay messages over a long

In order to help remember complicated songs filled with different rhythms and pitches, musicians created notes. These notes are like a musical language. Musicians who can read these notes can turn them into music. This lets musicians write their songs down for others to also play. As more pitches and rhythms were added, the notes became more advanced. It eventually became the standard notation of music seen today.

Historians believe the first musical instrument was the human voice.

You can be 48 blocks away and still hear a note block be played.

distance. Archaeologists have found instruments, like flutes, carved from bones—some over 41,000 years old!

Over time, this form of communication became a form of entertainment, as well. Music became a way for people to express their feelings. Early music was performed by memory. Nothing was written down. The music would be passed down from generation to generation. As time passed, however, people wanted to share music without having to perform it or remember how to play it.

Composers, people who write music, have used notation for hundreds of years to show how to perform their music. They

The earliest musical notations found are estimated to be more than 4,000 years old!

notate the music they have in their head to preserve the music exactly as they hear it. Composers have to decide the different rhythms and pitches they want to use. They also have to choose the tempo, which is the speed their music needs to be played, and the different instruments that will play their music.

You can be a composer in *Minecraft*. You can build a note block. These blocks can be built to create specific sounds when struck or powered by redstone. Note blocks can create different pitches. You can change the pitch to 24 different tones! You can even change the type of sound that a note block makes. Try placing different blocks under your note blocks to hear different instruments. If you put a gold block under a note block, it will sound like a bell. If you put a wool block under a note block, it will sound like a guitar. You can also change the length of the notes by using redstone repeaters. Try different combinations of these note blocks and redstone. You could consider adding a doorbell chime to your home or creating a theme song for your world. Or you could try to recreate your favorite song using note blocks. What other ideas and patterns of sounds can you create?

Will you recreate a song or create your own?

TECHNOLOGY

People have been recording events by writing them down for hundreds of years. These people were called **scribes**. They studied for up to 12 years to learn the skill of writing. (Not everyone could read and write in ancient times.) Scribes would record everyday experiences in writing. Over time, they copied the same written work over and over again. They did this to share the work with others. This need for copies created an opportunity for people to invent a way to **automate** the process of copying by hand.

Johannes Gutenberg, a German inventor, created a way to automate this process. Gutenberg's press used a stamp, paper, ink, and pressure to quickly make a copy of a work. The stamp was set in the press, and ink was put on the stamp. Paper was set over the stamp, and pressure was applied. The ink was transferred to the paper and then set out to dry. This process changed the way people copied words. The printing press revolutionized the way things were shared.

Scribes were considered powerful and important people across all cultures.

CHAPTER THREE

Interactive Art: Using All the Senses

Interactive art is meant to be experienced with all the senses, not just looked at or listened to. You may have encountered this type of art in your school or community. Does your school or community have a fountain in it? Fountains have been used for thousands of years as art pieces that also serve a real-world function, like providing easy access to water. In Islamic societies, people often built fountains outside their homes so travelers could get fresh water for their journey.

Some artists consider fountains as one of the earliest forms of interactive art. When you see a fountain, think about the designs and carvings you see, the sounds of the water flowing from the top, and the feel of the cool water. Try to build your own fountain in *Minecraft*. How can you design it to make it visually appealing? What materials can you use? Will it also be useful?

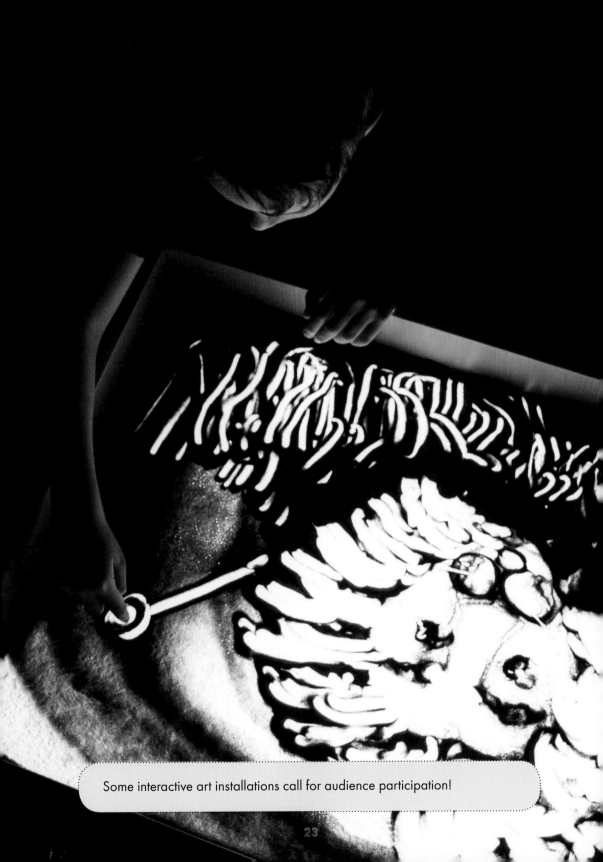

Some interactive art installations call for audience participation!

Interactive architecture is another type of art. It combines the visual, audible, and physical senses—and sometimes even the sense of smell! The ways you interact with the structure determines how the art will look. Each person will create their own art, and others will interpret that art differently. Interactive architecture goes beyond the standard ways of building. It incorporates the senses and invites the audience to move, touch, add to, and respond to it.

You can be an interactive artist in *Minecraft*. You can make interactive art by combining different blocks. You can use pressure plates to trigger blocks that create movement and sound when a visitor walks over them. You can also use sticky

You can see many examples of interactive art in communities around the world. One famous installation is the Heidelberg Project in Detroit, Michigan. Tyree Guyton, the creator of the Heidelberg Project, transformed an entire area of abandoned homes into visual art. The houses, yards, streetlights, and other parts of the neighborhood were all painted and turned into art you can see and walk through today. An example of musical interactive art is the Dithyrambalina. Many artists came together after Hurricane Katrina to turn old homes in New Orleans, Louisiana, into musical instruments to help uplift the local community.

Interactive art installations aren't just found in museums.

Some users incorporate animals into their art installation.

pistons to move blocks back and forth. This creates **dynamic** pieces of art that change as you interact with them. Movement is an important part of interactive art.

You can create the visual part of installation art in different ways. You can use glowstone and torches to add different brightness to your creations. Redstone ore will add an interactive element to your artwork because it **illuminates** when you walk over it. Levers and buttons can be used to light redstone torches, redstone lamps, and beacons. You can change the color of the light from a beacon by placing stained glass in the path of the light source. You can also use levers and buttons to trigger note blocks or sticky pistons.

Where will you add this type of art in your *Minecraft* world?

What will your interactive art installation look like?

Extension Activity

Think about how you can show your feelings and thoughts by building a piece of interactive art in *Minecraft*. First, think about the idea or feeling you want to show through your piece of art. Do you want to build a design for your family or friends? Do you want to build something based on how you feel today?

Then, design how your art will look. Will it be a small monument? Will it be large enough to walk through? Will it stand by itself or be built into a cave or other geographic feature? Will it have many parts or one big piece? Will it light up or be dark?

Next, think about what sounds your art will produce. Will you use the sounds of water to add a calming effect? Will you add note blocks and redstone for rhythm and pitch?

Once you have thought about those things, think about how people can interact with your art. Will you include levers and buttons people can pull or push to add effects or change the art? Will you add pistons and sticky pistons to make the artwork move as people step on pressure plates?

You can sketch your design ideas on paper first. Then you can create a small model of it in an area of *Minecraft* before you build your full piece of art.

Invite your *Minecraft* friends to visit your artwork. Ask for feedback!

Find Out More

Books

Gregory, Josh. *Minecraft : Guide to Building.* Ann Arbor, MI: Cherry Lake Publishing, 2017.

Jelley, Craig. *Minecraft : Guide to Creative.* New York: Del Rey, 2017.

Websites

The Cave Paintings at Lascaux

http://archeologie.culture.fr/lascaux/en

Take a virtual tour of the cave paintings in Lascaux, France. Read about the history of the site and why archaeologists think early humans created these cave paintings.

Composition Craft

https://files.Minecraftforge.net

A *Minecraft* mod designed by the University of Arkansas' Music Education and Tesseract programs teaches players how to compose and create music in a new and unique way.

Glossary

archaeologists (ahr-kee-AH-luh-jists) scientists who learn about the past by studying human-made objects found in the ground

audible (AW-duh-buhl) something you can hear

automate (AW-tuh-mate) to make something happen on its own or with only a little human input

domesticated (duh-MES-tih-kate-id) tamed (an animal) and made easier for humans to work with

dynamic (dye-NAM-ik) something that changes a lot or is full of energy

graffiti (gruh-FEE-tee) pictures or words drawn on surfaces such as walls, buses, and subway cars that are not supposed to be there

illuminates (ih-LOO-muh-nayts) lights up

intricate (IN-trih-kit) detailed

Paleolithic (pay-lee-oh-LITH-ik) a time when people only had stone tools to work with

scribes (SKRIBEZ) people who copied documents by hand before printing was invented

Index

Adam Hellebuyck is the dean of Curriculum and Assessment at University Liggett School in Grosse Pointe Woods, Michigan. Follow him on social media at @adamhellebuyck

Michael Medvinsky is the dean of Pedagogy and Innovation at University Liggett School in Grosse Pointe Woods, Michigan. Follow him on social media at @mwmedvinsky